LEADING
FROM THE GUT

3 Power Practices of Effective Leaders

TODD STOCKER

Cannon River Press
St. Paul * Houston
A Division of ToddStocker.com
www.toddstocker.com

© 2012, 2013 Todd Stocker. All rights reserved. No portion of this book may be reproduce, stored in a retrieval system, or transmitted in any form or by any means - electronic, mechanical, photocopy, recording, or any other - except for brief quotation in printed reviews, without the prior permission of the publisher.

Published by Cannon River Press, a Division of Todd Stocker.com, P.O. Box 25946, St. Paul, MN, 55125

All Scripture quotations, unless otherwise indicated, are taken from The Holy bible, New International Version (NIV). Copyright © 1973, 1978, 1984, International Bible Society. Used by permission of Zondervan Bible Publishers. Other Scripture references are from the following sources: The King James Version of the bible (KJV). The Message (MSG), copyright © 1993. Used by permission of NavPress Publishing Group. The Holy Bible, New Living Translation (NLT), copyright © 1996. Used by permission of Tyndale House Publishers, Inc., Wheaton, Illinois 60189. All rights reserved.

DEDICATED TO ALL THOSE WHO
KNOW THE IMPORTANCE OF LEADING
THEMSELVES FIRST

CONTENTS:

The Effects of Empty Leadership 7

Leadership Begins Below the Waterline 13

The Healthy Leaders Three GUT Principles 19

Conclusion 35

Author Bio and Contact Information.....................39

Other Books by Todd ……………………………..41

What Others Say ……………………………………44

Leading From The GUT

Todd Stocker

EVERYTHING
rises and falls on leadership
- John Maxwell

THE EFFECTS OF EMPTY LEADERSHIP

The introduction was lengthy and a bit uncomfortable. The emcee listed several of my accomplishments and my job title which was more than a bit exaggerated. When he was done, the crowd clapped enthusiastically and starred at the empty stage. I was behind the curtains.

Soon the clapping faded and still the stage was empty. I heard the murmuring and everyone felt that uncomfortable air that something had gone wrong. "Did he forget? Did he hear the intro?

Did he pass out? Maybe he's in the bathroom!" I slowly walked on stage, walked to one side of middle and said, "In the absence of leadership, people get nervous." The point was made. As I continued my seminar, there was that sense of relief to know that someone was doing something, something was happening, and momentum pushed through the stale uncomfortableness of the empty stage.

It is true, isn't it? When our projects, teams or events fail, sometimes it is the fault of external circumstances but most often, the error can be traced back to weak or absent leadership. John Maxwell said, "Everything rises and falls on Leadership."

Without leadership, people are left with confusion and uncertainty. Without leadership, people fill in the gaps with no direction or purpose.

My Leadership Break-through
or rather: Break-apart

When I was in grade school, I realized I was not and probably wouldn't be the most popular kid. I was a non-athletic, chubby kid who loved to play piano and be in the background. For some reason, the popular kids in school liked that about me, even though I wasn't like them. They invited me to come over and play in their yards and just hang out.

Secretly, I'd always want to be popular like them, but what I didn't realize was that I was popular, in a different way. I didn't get the girls. I didn't get the attention. But even as a kid, I noticed that when I didn't want to do what everyone else was doing, eventually the other kids were doing what I wanted to do and was doing already, instead! (You may need to re-read that last sentence).

As I grew and developed, I was somewhat of a success at what I did. Getting jobs was not hard for me and promotions came as second nature. I was in the Customer Service industry for most of my working life, starting out as a front desk clerk at small local hotel be being a manager at a resort in the exclusive foothills of Phoenix. From there I went from being a Customer Service Representative at America West (now US AIR) to helping with training new employees. I also did a stint at American Express where I went from being a "phone-jockey" to being an Operations Trainer.

I have led small, two person companies and organizations in the thousands. But my biggest leadership learning lesson came when I was leading a church/organization of a few hundred people. At that point, everything on the surface of my life glittered. I had just come from a church that was the fastest growing (percentage-wise) in our state denomination. I had a great salary, supportive team and "success" was my passenger.

On the surface, it looked as if I were living my dream. I had the money, I had the fame, I had the girls (my wife and daughters). On the outside my life looked great. But on the inside, I was dying. Somehow I knew that I couldn't keep up the pace and that the exterior was simply a veneer for what was crumbling inside of me.

My breaking point came one night after a long, hard day. After dinner, I went out on our back deck to make a fire in our outdoor fireplace. Suddenly, I found myself crying uncontrollably. Tears flooded in, out and down my cheeks and I didn't know why. For hours, I sat there staring into the flames and I pondered how I'd sunk to the point of being fake on the outside and empty on the inside.

At around 2am, the fire died down and I was sound asleep on my deck-chair. Waking up with the sun, I immediately cancelled my whole day and went to the seaside where I, again, walked through the hallways of my life, trying to find a reason - any reason - for my breakdown.

Finally, it dawned on me. I was pouring everything out into everyone else and nothing was coming back into me. I was empty because I didn't manage the inside of me, only the outside. Things had to change and thankfully, they did.

LEADERSHIP
and learning are indispensable
to each other.
- John F. Kennedy

LEADERSHIP BEGINS BENEATH THE "WATERLINE"

If I were to ask you to describe someone you know that you thought was a great leader, what would you say? Most likely, you would describe that persons skills, style, personality, drive and a plethora of other characteristics. But leadership is more that what we see a person do. Leadership is who a person is. I learned that lesson the hard way.

There are two realities of leadership. The first has to do with the skills, strategy, and methods of leading or managing. It is what people see us do. Making decisions, casting vision, leading problem solving are all part of doing leadership.

The second has to do with the heart or character of a leader. In the Bible it says that if anyone wants to be a leader, they must first watch their own life. They must have control over their emotions, have a servant mindset and take time for solitude. (Titus 1). This is what I was missing and what is the most important part of your leadership.

In your mind, picture a sailboat. It is floating on the peaceful ocean a few feet from shore with seagulls hovering above it's white, flowing mast. The shiny wood deck glistens from the soft morning mist and it's riggings are ready to go.

That was the scene me and 15 other men experienced the second morning of a leadership workshop in Corpus Christi, TX. Part of the workshop was to have an "out of the box" experience, something that we'd normally not do.

Our captain had been sailing since he was a kid and gave us basic instructions. Simply put, he said, "listen and do what I say… that's it."

We headed out across the bay. Suddenly, the boat lurched to a stop cause most of us to instinctively grab hold of whatever or whomever was nearby. We had hit a submerged sandbar a few hundred yards of the coastline.

Immediately, our captain began barking orders lest we tip and sink. He had us go to one side of the boat then the other, shifting the weight to pry us free from the underwater sand. He also had us jump on the count of three to force the weight down then up. It worked and we were off into the water. Later, I spoke to the captain about the experience and he said that often times, sailors get caught up in looking at the sails but forget about the most important part of the ship. That "most-important" part is what they sometimes call the "guts."

That experience illustrates what good leadership is about. Long term effective leadership begins with what is not seen in public. It is what is beneath the waterline. It is the guts. It is what is inside. It can make or break you as a leader.

The "guts" of your leadership needs to be weightier than what is on the outside. My captain said that without a good balance under the water, the ship is easily pushed over. In leadership you can take this truth to the bank. History has thousands of illustrations of fallen leaders. Fallen not because of being externally out-pace, but internally weak. Often healthy leadership is hard to see.

The boat metaphor makes me think that that is why we call it Leader-*ship*.

I was reading an article about a great leader named Dee Hock. He is the man who first conceived of a global system for the electronic exchange of value, becoming the founder and CEO of VISA International. In the article, Dee talks about the fatal move of first thinking about those whom you are leading. From many years of successful leadership he states,

"The first and paramount responsibility of anyone who purports to manage is to manage self: one's own integrity, character, ethics, knowledge, wisdom, temperament, words and acts."

He goes on to suggest that good leaders use a certain percentage of their time in leading oneself.

"Control is not leadership; management is not leadership; leadership is leadership. If you seek to lead, invest at least 50% of your time in

leading yourself—your own purpose, ethics, principles, motivation, conduct.

Did you catch that? 50% managing his or herself so that they bring a full heart into their leadership responsibilities.

Frank Vandersloot, Founder and CEO of The Melaleuca Wellness Company said, "You need to be a leader on all levels of your life." Start with what's beneath your waterline.

the first person I will ever lead
- John Maxwell

THE THREE GUT PRACTICES

My dismal life condition years ago can, to a large degree, be attributed to spending too much time managing those under my care and very little managing my heart.

Maybe you find that true of you today. Way to many leaders have hearts that are in trouble even though they continue to show up and fulfill their leadership responsibilities. Dan Webster, in an article titled "Lead Yourself First," says that leaders whose hearts are in trouble and whose leadership guts may be sinking show it in various ways. He says that a heart that is flatlined (or *sinking* to use our metaphor) can't feel deep emotion anymore and that there is a numbness that keeps it from "beating." That kind of heart also doesn't have room for laughter or spontaneity and has lost it's ability to have compassion for those who are hurting.

I remember when I was at that low point in my leadership journey, a friend called and asked if he could talk me to lunch to talk about the pain he was experiencing as he went through a nasty divorce. My first thought - and I'm embarrassed to admit this - was, "Great, FREE LUNCH." My leadership heart had sunk and I had no compassion whatsoever.

Does that describe you today? Are you pouring your whole energy into others and forgetting to tend to that which is unseen - below the waterline? Do you feel that you're just dialing in your leadership and feel that you are just a shell of who you once were?

Pastor Rick Warren says, "My nose is prominent but not important. My guts are important but not prominent." To be a good leader, you need to lead yourself first and tend to the unseen, important part of you - YOU!

Those who survive and thrive in life learn what it means to be renewed so that they bring a fresh self into their work and relationships. In the next section, we'll describe how to LEAD FROM YOUR GUT.

The first step in any journey is to take the first step. However, that first step doesn't (or shouldn't) happen until you commit to the adventure. To keep your leadership sails filled with air, make sure you are committed to being a healthy and growing leader and not simply going through the motions. Once you do that, you are now ready to move to "shore up the hold" and become the best leader you can be.

Using an acronym, let's examine three principles for leading from the G.U.T.

G: GIVE YOURSELF A GUT-CHECK

I read a report that talked about something called our "2nd Physical Brain." It stated that unknown to most people, we actually have two physical brains. You're intimately familiar with the brain encased in your skull but did you know you also have a second brain in your gut? Scientists call it our Enteric Nervous System.

This gut-brain and your skull-brain developed from the same embryonic cell cluster and contains over one half of your nerve cells. Your gut-brain is also able to learn, remember, and produce emotion-based feelings. That's why the expression "gut-level feeling" isn't just a "saying." We really do have feelings in our gut!

If emotions are stored in our gut, it is vitally important that we are taking time to evaluate how we are "feeling." Good leaders have that feeling of confidence, calmness and control. Here are a few questions to help:

1) How are your GUTS today? How are you really? Any signs of trouble?

2) Do you have a plan for addressing and tending to any emotional issues? When will you make one?

3) What can you do this weekend that will renew you and be fun?

4) When will you get alone and quiet in the next 24 hours?

Another tie to good leadership and our gut is simply this - eat right and stay healthy! We all know that feeling of running from one meeting to another, grabbing fast food in between and feeling lethargic and unable to think for the rest of the day.

Within recent months, I lost 45 pounds and am maintaining a healthy weight. I am more focused, more productive and I have more energy that I know what to do with. If you want to know how I did it, you can order my book, "Break Through Weight Loss" at my website (www.ToddStocker.com)

Make a plan.   Eat healthy.   Your stomach, emotions and life will thank you for it.

U: UTILIZE OTHERS
One of the key hallmarks of good leadership is the ability of the leader to delegate to her team. Authoritative delegation is what gets things done in any organization and has a drastic affect and the leaders effectiveness.

So why would I include it as something that is "below the waterline?"   Simply because the personal effect of good delegation is drastically understated.

Most of us are not good delegators. We take on too much. We have a need to be in control. We believe that no one can do it better than ourselves and as a result, we spend extra time doing tasks that others could do. Doing too much takes too much time and leads to burn out. And not many leaders recover when they've truly burnt out.

So how do you utilize others? The two that I've found effective personally and that I've coached others in are these:
1) Consistently prioritize what you are doing.
2) Build strong teams.

EXAMINE WHAT YOU'RE DOING:
Make a list of everything you do or are responsible for.
Place a "1" by the activities that only you can do.
Place a "2" by the activities that you or someone else could do.
Place a "3" by the activities that you don't have to do at all.

Now the hard part. Take items marked "2" and ask the question, "To whom could I share or hand this off. I included *sharing* because the "2's" on your list may be activities that you need to have a small level of hand's on investment. The "3's" simply need to be delegated to someone else. For entrepreneurial leaders, most often this is administrative tasks but it could be a product line that you don't need to oversee. I know the president of a large company who still feels the need to sign purchase orders under a small dollar amount. Hand it off! You'll feel better and your gut will love you!

BUILD AN ALL-STAR TEAM:

I learned how to build teams years ago when starting a church/organization outside of Phoenix. As any entrepreneur, I quickly became the CEO and janitor in a few short days. As we grew, I knew that I needed to build a team or else I'd implode.

I learned a model on which I've adapted over the years that is simple, Biblical and very, very effective! I call it the All-Star model and I've used it to help leaders on all levels - even Moms and Dads!

I teach a seminar called "HOW TO BUILD AN ALL STAR TEAM" and you can find out more by going to my website at www.ToddStocker.com and click "speaking." But below is the basic overview and then an example of the star.

1. Draw 5 point star.
2. In the center of the star, write the name of the team, it's purpose and who is the point leader.
3. Title the bottom 4 arms and provide a description of what each arm would be doing. (The top arm is your role and you'll fill that in later). When you're done with these 4, ask yourself, "Does everything about my event, department or activity fit into one of these 4?" If not, think at a higher level.

4. Now, title your arm, the top one. Describe what your role would be. In my seminars I always encourage the point person to write in "provides visionary leadership" because that is your main job.
5. Determine what *type* of person you want in each arm. DO NOT think of individuals just yet. In this step you're asking, "What kind of person do I want doing this kind of task? Do I need a detailed person or someone who is also good with people? Do I need someone who can build another team under them if necessary or someone who simply can get the job done themselves?" I also include if this job would be better suited for an outgoing personality or better for someone who likes to work behind the scenes.
6. Now, think of names of people who would first, fit each task and second, that you could see working together as an All-Star Team. I ask, "Do they have the giftedness necessary to complete the job? Do they have a passion for that area? Do they have experience

already in this area?" I encourage thinking of at least two people and prioritize them based on your top pick then work down.

And now the most important step…

7. ASK! You now need to ask the people who you've identified on each to be on your team! This is where leadership goes from theory to application. If you don't make 'the ask' then you might as well not even start the process.

I've used this little model in almost every team environment. When I'm planning speaking or seminars I first ask, "How can I build a team around this event or experience," and then I launch into the above exercise. It has helped me be more organized and allows for more to get done through other people.

Great leaders realize that more can be done and be done better when the load is shared. So utilize others to create a balanced leader-*ship*.

To review:
>G: Give yourself a Gut-check.
>U: Utilize others.

T: TAKE TIME FOR SOLITUDE
Solitude is defined as the state or position of being alone. This is one of the most important activities for leaders and yet, the most neglected. Taking time to be peaceful and reflective resets your leadership compass. Solitude gets you in touch with yourself and with God. In fact, great things happen when you change up the scenery, get away or simply invest the time to rest.

Great leaders throughout history engaged in the practice of solitude. One of my favorite leaders is King David. Here was a little boy who took care of sheep for a living and yet went on to do great things. He was the on the other end of the slingshot that launched the stone that killed Goliath. He also led the charge and conquered the city of Jerusalem, set up a dynasty through a covenant and united the north and south into a single kingdom. On top of all that, he was a prolific musician and poet!

How did he accomplish so much and yet keep his sanity? One of his "secrets" was that he took time away to be refreshed. In fact, he would spend a healthy chunk of time during the most stressful times to be with God and seek his council. In 2 Samuel 22:20, David says that "God brought me out into a spacious place." It was in that open space that David gained perspective and direction for his next move.

The point in all of this is that you were designed to take time to be refreshed. You need times away and times to regroup.

I've heard it said that "life is a marathon." I don't believe that sentiment. I believe that life is a series of sprints, in between which you need to slow down to prepare for the next battle.

There is a phrase that one leader told me during my melt-down which has proved to be very helpful:

"Divert daily, withdraw weekly, retreat monthly and abandon annually"

<u>Divert Daily:</u> Take a break from your normal routine. 12-14 hours is too long to be focused on one type of work.

<u>Withdraw Weekly:</u> Find a place that you can spend time doing an activity that refreshes you. For me, it's outdoors or in a quiet spot to do some writing.

<u>Move Monthly:</u> Pull away from the grind and change your setting. I've loved to take a day tarrying along the aisles in antique stores in river towns like Hudson or Stillwater.

<u>Abandon Annually:</u> I try to pack a bag and hide away for an extended period in a cabin or some other place completely removed from familiarity.

I'm a spiritual man and so in these times, God meets me. He encourages me. He gives me direction and strength. For me, that is the secret to being a healthy, long-lasting leader.

Leading From The GUT

LEADERS
change the world,
one life at a time,
starting with their own.
- Todd Stocker

CONCLUSION:
WE ARE HUMAN **BEINGS** FIRST
NOT HUMAN **DOINGS**.

A friend of mine was on the outer edges of burnout. He was productive in what he felt called to do but was over-worked and under-healthy. He had decided to quit but thought it best to see a counselor before he did. At the appointment, the counselor asked, "Do you have a garden?" My friend was stumped. Of course not! He was too busy, too depressed, and too exhausted. "That is your problem." said the counselor. "Your whole life is wrapped around your duties and you have nothing that is yours to which you can attend. Plant a garden and you'll survive."

So, he bought a "garden-in-a-box" and set up the 2 foot by 2 foot crate on his back deck. After three days, little shoots came up to which he tended. After a week, the garden was flourishing with sprouts from different herbs and small tomato plants poking their stems up from beneath the dirt. Today, my friend accredits that little plot to saving his marriage, saving his job and saving his life. Why? Because the garden was something that he could do that no one else saw and that refreshed him below his "waterline."

All of us go through times when we are feeling empty, depressed and overwhelmed. It is simply part of our human experience. But wise leaders are intentional about attending to what is below the waterline.

Make sure you don't get blown over by the winds of responsibility. Make sure you're checking the waters of your leadership and make sure you're as intentional in leading yourself as you are in leading others. As you do, you'll become a more healthy, long-lasting leader who help to change the world, one life at a time!

Leading From The GUT

WHOEVER

wants to become great among you must be your Servant.
- Matthew 20:26

ABOUT THE AUTHOR:
TODD STOCKER

is a speaker, author and Pastor. For more than 15 years, Todd has been helping people in non-profit organizations and businesses understand that personal leadership is a key to a more fulfilled and successful life.

A nationally sought after communicator and winner of the Rickman Award for Creative Communication, Todd has been the keynote speaker at business conferences, seminars, youth camps, and men's and women's ministry events. Todd is the author of "Infinite Playlists" and "Dancing with God", "Refined - Turning Pain into Purpose." He and his family live in Woodbury, Minnesota. For more information, you can go to www.toddstocker.com

"MY PERSONAL MISSION is to honor God by adding value and leadership to the lives of people around me. Through creative communication and innovative resourcing, I will help facilitate positive life change in my personal relationships and throughout the world."
-Todd Stocker

Also Available from
TODD STOCKER

"**REFINED** - *Turning Pain Into Purpose.*" Todd had the perfect life. All of it was interrupted when his oldest daughter was killed in a traffic accident. "REFINED," examines principles that help answer the questions that surface when pain and tragedy poke their noses into our lives. Whether you have experienced the tragic loss of a loved one or struggle with the daily frustrations of life, "REFINED" will help you understand what God may be up to.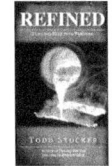

"**DANCING WITH GOD** – *First Year Thoughts on the Loss of My Daughter.*" All of us go through loss. This incredibly emotional book chronicles the year following an accident that killed Todd's oldest daughter. Join him on his journey of loss as he was *comforted by the Lord in amazing and powerful ways.*

"MANNERS MATTER – *10 Table Manners Every Child Should Know."* Eating a meal together as a family can be a wonderful opportunity for building closer relationships and having fun at the same time! Our book, "Manners Matter" can help begin conversation with your youngster about proper table manners and why they are important.

"INFINITE PLAYLISTS – *How to have Conversations, not Conflict, with your Child about Music."* This is a handy guide to healthy conversation between parents and kids. Writing as both father and music-lover, Todd calls parents to recognize music as a gift from God so they can help their kids determine the emotional, physical, and spiritual influences of their song choices. He offers a balanced look at the difference between Christian and secular music, and gives practical guidelines parents and kids can follow to choose appropriate music-together.

For more information and to invite Todd to speak at your event,
GO TO
www.ToddStocker.com

Cannon River Press
St. Paul * Houston
A Division of ToddStocker.com
www.toddstocker.com

WHAT OTHERS SAY ...

"I was so confused about our Business Student Organization event but after working through the All-Star Model, I have a clear direction and am excited to build a healthy, efficient team. Thanks!"   - Nicole Zastrow, Concordia University, St. Paul

"While all of the speakers were inspirational, I especially enjoyed the message that Todd gave on Friday afternoon. At the end of the very emotional message, it was as though Todd was talking directly to us when he said, "As for you who are thinking about quitting, DON'T!" - Mark & Angela Leefe, Texas

"It was so great to come away from this presentation and feel energized — like I could take on the world! Thank you, Todd!" – Margaret Vennering, St. Paul, MN

"I have had so many positive comments about last weekend. I want you to now that you connected well with a young mom. After your message, she realized she needed to make some changes in her relationships. Thanks again!" - Pastor Bill Hugo

"I am so grateful for Todd's feedback and his training was some of the best coaching I've ever had!" - Pastor Derek Broten

"Todd was very professional and interesting. What he taught us about living and working 'stress-less' will help me in my personal and work world!" – Jeff Bacci, Tomball, TX

"I liked the humor during the presentation. It really kept me engaged and I learned so much about balancing life and work." - Gail Stephanoski, Spring, TX

www.ingramcontent.com/pod-product-compliance
Lightning Source LLC
Chambersburg PA
CBHW051823170526
45167CB00005B/2138